Deal with your Feelings and Flourish

A guide to navigate your emotions and adapt to uncertainties

Garry M. Hall

Contents

Introduction

Why Is It Important to Manage Your feelings?

Consider that your master and a couple of your associates are at a meeting with you. After months of active labor, you're ready to showcase your design's findings and solicit feedback. You're certain that you did a fantastic job since you took the time to produce a thorough report and an engaging donation. You launch into your speech with clarity and vigor, but soon you catch your master glooming and shaking his head. He frequently interrupts you with critical reflections and inquiries while appearing to disregard your ideas and suggestions. Your face flushes, and you feel your heart pounding. You begin to question your capacities and your work. You witness rage and frustration. You want to stand up for yourself and falsify him, but you also want to be calm and avoid a fight. How would you handle this dilemma? How do you manage your studies, passions, and conduct?

This is only one of the innumerous circumstances that test our passions on a diurnal base. Our lives aren't complete without feelings. They've an impact on our stations, choices, conduct, interpersonal relations, health, and happiness. They can also lead to difficulty, conflict, pressure, and confusion. Success in both our particular and professional lives can be greatly impacted by how we handle our feelings.

The capability to maneuver your inner terrain with inflexibility and moxie is dealing with passions. It entails being suitable to admit, accept, and comprehend your feelings without allowing them to rule your conduct. It also involves being suitable to bear in a way that's harmonious with your points and values, despite challenges or unknowns.

It doesn't include giving in to or ignoring your feelings, nor does it involve savoring or expressing them. Chancing a formative balance between your passions and your geste is the thing. It involves using your feelings as a source of knowledge and alleviation rather than as roadblocks or apologies.

For everyone who wishes to succeed in moment's complex and changing world, the capacity to manage one's feelings is a pivotal skill. It can help you in:

- Boost your effectiveness and performance at work

- Boost your interpersonal chops and cooperation
- Increase your resiliency and general good
- Develop your innovative and creative thinking
- Promote your own particular development

I will explain to you in this book how to use the rules and ways for managing your feelings in a variety of circumstances. I will also tell you some stories about people who crushed obstacles and fulfilled their objects by being emotionally nimble. What you'll learn to do is;

1. Avoid the hazards of repressing or overreacting to your feelings by understanding the nature and function of your feelings.
2. Admit and understand your feelings

3. Put some distance between your passions and your geste

4. Align your geste with your values and objects.

5. Reframe your issues and alter your point of view.

6. Develop tone-compassion and adaptability

7. Speak easily and sympathize with others

8. Be flexible and open to misgivings

You can manage your feelings and thrive in every situation by perfecting your emotional inflexibility. You will be suitable to have a further gratified and meaningful life.

Chapter 1

The Origin and Purpose of Emotion

Describe emotions. How are they created? How do they behave? These are some of the issues that will be covered in this chapter. Subjective feelings, physiological changes, cognitive assessments, and behavioral manifestations all play a part in the complexity of emotions. Emotions have essential purposes and significance for our survival and well-being; they are not random or senseless.

I.   The Origin of Emotion

Emotions are frequently described as multidimensional structures made up of four parts:

1. **Subjective feelings:** These are the emotional states that we are aware of and categorize as joy, anger, fear, sadness, etc. Our personalities, moods, and cultures all have an impact on our subjective feelings.

2. **Physiological changes:** These are the physical manifestations of emotion, such as heightened breathing, blood pressure, sweating, and hormonal production. The autonomic nerve system and the endocrine system mediate physiological changes that position us for action.

3. **Cognitive appraisals:** These are the assessments and interpretations we give to the things that make us feel something. Our beliefs, expectations, aspirations, values, and attributions are all a part of cognitive appraisals. The kind and degree

of emotion we feel is determined by cognitive evaluations.

4. **Behavioral expressions:** These are the outward displays of emotion that humans make, such as smiling, frowning, sobbing, shouting, or running away. Behaviors help us express our feelings to others and shape their responses.

These four elements of emotion interact and have an impact on one another. For instance, both our physiological changes and our subjective feelings might influence one another. Our behavioral manifestations can be influenced by our cognitive judgments and vice versa. Additionally, these elements might vary in length and intensity based on the circumstance and the person.

II.   The Purpose of Emotion

Emotions perform a variety of vital tasks in our lives. Several of these include:

- **Adaptive function:** By inspiring us to work toward our goals and stay away from dangers, emotions aid in our ability to adapt to our surroundings. For instance, anger aids in the defense of oneself or one's rights, while happiness aids in the pursuit of possibilities for development and reward.

- **Social function:** Emotions facilitate social interaction by communicating our goals, desires, and preferences to others. For instance, melancholy indicates that we require assistance or support, disgust indicates that we despise something or someone, and love indicates that we regard and care for another person.

- **Communicative function:** Emotions aid in persuasion by evoking sympathy, empathy, or cooperation in others. For instance, remorse inspires others to extend forgiveness or make amends, gratitude inspires them to show loyalty or reciprocity, and pride inspires them to show respect or adoration.

- **Regulatory function:** By offering feedback and direction, emotions assist us in controlling our own behavior. For instance, guilt motivates us to make amends or better ourselves, curiosity piques our interest in learning new things and developing new talents, and boredom motivates us to look for novelty or change.

Our psychological health depends on our ability to experience emotions. They make life more enjoyable by giving our encounters context and flavor. They also put us to the test by forcing us to deal with challenges and uncertainty. We can improve our emotional agility and make informed emotional decisions by comprehending the nature and purpose of emotion.

Chapter 2

Emotional management techniques

There are numerous efficient and healthy methods for handling your emotions. Among them are:

Deep breathing

When you feel anxious or overwhelmed, this might help you relax and regulate your nervous system. Until you feel more at ease, try breathing for four counts, holding for four counts, then exhaling for four counts.

Grounding techniques

These can assist you in maintaining your attention in the present moment rather than allowing your thoughts or feelings to take over.

Try singing or humming, spraying cold water on your face, or practicing the progressive muscle relaxation technique, which involves tensing and relaxing various muscle groups throughout your body.

Mindfulness

This might assist you in seeing and accepting your feelings without opposing them or passing judgment on them. You might try paying attention to your emotions, the ideas and sensations that go along with them, and what your emotions are attempting to tell you. You can also engage in mindfulness meditation, in which you pay attention to your breath or a mantra and gently draw it back if it veers away.

Acceptance

This can assist you in validating and recognizing your emotions rather than repressing or denying them. You may try telling yourself that it's acceptable to feel this way. Although I don't have to like it, I can deal with it. My feelings are fleeting; they will vanish. You might also try journaling, creating art or music, or writing down your feelings.

Thought challenging

This can assist you in recognizing and refuting any erroneous or distorted thoughts that could set off or exacerbate your emotional reactions. Try examining your thoughts by asking yourself, "Is this notion founded on facts or assumptions? Is there an alternative perspective on this matter? What would I tell a friend who was thinking this? You can also attempt substituting more realistic and optimistic thoughts with negative ones.

Support for mental health

This can assist you in getting expert advice and support for managing your emotions, particularly if they are interfering with your ability to function or your general well-being. Try speaking with a therapist, counselor, coach, or other mental health professional who can support you emotionally and teach you coping mechanisms. They can also assist you in understanding the causes and implications of your emotions.

Utilizing these techniques can help you become more adept at controlling your emotions, which will enhance your mental health, wellbeing, and quality of life. Understanding and managing your emotions as a natural part of who you are, rather than trying to control or avoid them, is the better approach.

Chapter 3

Benefits of managing your emotions

Emotions play a crucial role in the human experience and have a profound effect on our health, conduct, and interpersonal relationships. Therefore, rather than ignoring, repressing, or avoiding our emotions, it is crucial to deal with them in a healthy and appropriate manner. The following are some advantages of managing your emotions:

1. **Increasing your mental well-being and resiliency:** You can lower your risk of acquiring emotional disorders like anxiety or depression by accepting and acknowledging your emotions.

Additionally, you can improve your capacity to handle pressure, difficulty, and change.

2. **Improving your physical health and performance:** You can improve your blood pressure, heart rate, and cortisol levels by managing and expressing your emotions. You can also increase your energy levels, productivity, and immune system.

3. **Increasing your self-esteem and self-assurance:** You can create a more positive and accurate self-image by realizing and recognizing your feelings. Additionally, you can improve your level of self-knowledge, self-compassion, and self-efficacy.

4. **Developing your interpersonal communication, conflict resolution, and collaboration abilities:** You can do this by communicating and empathizing with your emotions. You can also strengthen your relationships and trust with other people.

5. **Enhancing your personal development and happiness:** You can learn new things about yourself and your potential by examining and expressing your feelings. Additionally, you can live a life that is more meaningful and fulfilling.

You may improve every part of your life by learning to better manage your emotions. You should value and celebrate your emotions as a part of who you are rather than being ashamed or afraid of them.

Chapter 4

Overcoming Typical Obstacles to Handling Your Emotions

It might be difficult to deal with your emotions for a variety of reasons. The following are some typical obstacles that could make it difficult for you to adequately manage your emotions:

Fear

You might be terrified of experiencing your emotions, particularly if they are unpleasant, strange, or painful. You can be concerned that your emotions would control you, injure you, or cause you to lose it. You can worry that by expressing your emotions, others will judge you, reject you, or criticize you.

Shame

If your feelings are unfavorable, strong, or improper, you could feel ashamed of them. You might believe your emotions are incorrect, undesirable, or weak. You can also feel embarrassed about needing assistance or support to manage your emotions.

Habit

You may have developed unhealthy or ineffective coping mechanisms for your emotions, such as avoiding, denying, or numbing them. These habits may have been formed as a result of past trauma, abuse, or neglect. These behaviors could have also been ingrained in you by your family, community, or society.

Skill deficiency

You might lack the abilities or resources necessary to manage your emotions well. You can be unable to recognize, comprehend, accept, express, or control your feelings. You could also be unsure of how to get professional assistance or support for your emotional problems.

You may find it challenging to manage your emotions because of these obstacles, but they are not insurmountable. The following actions can help you get through them:

❖ Recognize and confront your fears: Try to face and explore your feelings rather than ignoring or running from them. Ask yourself what and why you are afraid. Present facts and data to refute any illogical or excessive fears. Remind yourself that you can manage your emotions and that they are normal and natural.

❖ Develop and use self-compassion: Try to be understanding and kind to yourself rather than criticizing or blaming yourself for your feelings. Realize that your feelings don't define who you are or what you're worth. Be kind to yourself as you would a friend going through a difficult period. Accept responsibility for any errors or shortfalls.

❖ Break and replace your habits: Try to develop new and better ways to deal with your emotions rather than relying on harmful or ineffective coping mechanisms. Determine the causes, effects, and effects on you and others of your habits. Replace them with coping mechanisms that are healthier and more powerful, like those described above.

* Learn and use new skills: Try to learn and use new skills and tools to better regulate your emotions rather than feeling helpless or hopeless about them. Look for credible sources of knowledge and instruction regarding emotional control and wellbeing. Consult a therapist, counselor, coach, or other mental health professional for professional assistance or support who can give you emotional support and new skills.

* You can remove the obstacles that stand in your way of efficiently managing your emotions by following these steps. Additionally, you can enhance your emotional wellbeing, quality of life, and health. You should accept and value your

emotions as a part of who you are rather than being afraid or ashamed of them.

Chapter 5

Applying emotional intelligence in various contexts

The capacity to comprehend and control both your own and other people's emotions is known as emotional intelligence (EI). Your performance, well-being, and interpersonal and occupational relationships can all be improved with EI. EI can be used in a variety of contexts, including:

At work

EI can support productive communication, productive collaboration, constructive conflict resolution, and effective leadership. By actively and empathically listening to your coworkers and clients, providing and receiving constructive criticism, expressing gratitude and recognition, adapting to shifting circumstances and demands, controlling stress and emotions, inspiring and motivating others, and fostering a supportive work environment, you can use EI in the workplace.

At home

EI can encourage your loved ones, strengthen family ties, and help you deal with difficulties. Spending quality time with your family, expressing interest and curiosity in their lives, sharing your feelings and needs, respecting their feelings and needs, resolving conflicts amicably and respectfully, offering support and encouragement, and commemorating accomplishments and milestones are all ways you can practice emotional intelligence at home.

In the classroom

EI can support successful learning, academic success, and a positive social environment. By paying attention and participating in class, asking for assistance when necessary, managing your time and tasks, dealing with pressure and expectations, handling failure and setbacks, cooperating and collaborating with peers and teachers, respecting diversity and differences, and participating in extracurricular activities, you can apply EI in the classroom.

In the community

EI can assist you in making a difference, giving back to society, and interacting with people. EI can be used in the community by doing things like volunteering for a cause that matters to you, joining an interest-based club or group, going to events or activities that enrich you, networking and forming relationships with people who share your values or aspirations, speaking out for causes that are important to you, respecting the rights and opinions of others, and acting as a good citizen.

You may improve every area of your life by using EI in various contexts. EI is a skill that you can learn and hone with practice rather than a set quality that you either have or don't. Emotions are a resource and an advantage that can help you reach your potential rather than a barrier or a diversion.

Conclusion

Being able to manage your emotions is crucial to have a happy life. Emotions are natural and typical reactions to your ideas, encounters, and circumstances. They provide you helpful advice, recommendations, and criticism. But emotions can sometimes be difficult and overpowering, particularly if they are strong, frequent, or contradictory. As a result, it's crucial to manage your emotions in a healthy and productive way. Here are some suggestions for daily emotional management practice:

Recognize your emotions

Acknowledging and naming your feelings is the first step in coping with them. You can achieve this by paying attention to your bodily sensations, thoughts, and behaviors; identifying your emotions using a feelings wheel or a journal; considering the causes and implications of your emotions; and embracing your emotions without opposing or condemning them.

Communicate your feelings

Having a healthy and suitable means to communicate your emotions is the second step in dealing with them. You can achieve this by being honest and respectful, choosing the appropriate setting, person, and time to express your feelings, using "I" statements to convey your requirements, avoiding personal attacks on others, and utilizing nonverbal indicators like eye contact, tone of voice, and body language.

Regulate your emotions

Managing your emotions well and coping with stress are the third and last steps in dealing with them. You can achieve this by: recognizing and challenging any distorted or irrational thoughts; utilizing self-talk and positive affirmations; practicing relaxation techniques like yoga, deep breathing, or meditation; partaking in physical activity; asking for support when needed; and setting reasonable, attainable goals.

Learn from your emotions

This is the fourth step in handling your emotions; use them as a resource. Asking yourself what your emotions are trying to tell you, looking into the meaning and purpose of your emotions, seeing the positive elements or opportunities in your emotions, finding ways to express or create based on your emotions, and celebrating or enjoying them are all ways to do this.

You may enhance your emotional wellbeing, quality of life, and emotional health by regularly practicing how to manage your emotions. Embracing and appreciating your emotions as a part of who you are is better than fearing or avoiding them.